Seas

To Jill: that hidden strength that creates a wave and accompanies it right onto the beach.

One day, while reading the lyrics to my songs, and mindful of my nickname, "the poet of song writing", Jill suggested I make them into a book of poetry by simply taking out any repetitions of the chorus.

This book is the result.

© 2013 Lou Pizzi All rights reserved

Front & back covers: painting by Lou Pizzi
© Lou Pizzi 2008

Translated from Italian into English by Jill Vance

ISBN: 978-1-291-40299-5
eBook ISBN: 978-1-291-40320-6

ISBN in Italian: 978-1-291-54877-8
eBook ISBN in Italian: 978-1-291-54887-7

Author's Note

In writing this book I started collecting all the poems and songs I had written, and it was only then I saw a pattern emerging.

The beginning of my life was full of hope, expectations and journeys of discovery – 'Spring'.

I got a job, got married and started the conventional life expected of me. This clipped the wings of my imagination and pulled me into 'Autumn', passing summer by.

Only by rereading some of my poems did I see the amount of discontent, and realised there were things that needed to change. It was time to leave 'Winter' behind.

Divorce, quitting the job and throwing caution to the wind followed. These in turn led to my meeting the person that should have been in my life from the beginning, and who encouraged me to live my dreams – 'Summer'.

I have completed the circle and am back to journeys of discovery and joy. I am now a poet, songwriter and painter, and, according to my partner this is what I was born to be.

I do not know where these seasons come from – whether we create them ourselves, or if they are indeed brought by the wind. I have travelled all four and am waiting to see what the wind brings next.

Spring

The Flight of a Seagull	P 6
Invisible Hand	P 9
When the Sky is Calm	P 11
The Part Shadowed by the Sun	P 12
Night Time	P 13
Dear Old Story	P 15
I Know	P 17
When the Sun Shines	P 18
When	P 20
Tell Me About You	P 21
Something is There	P 22
My Seasons	P 23
Colours of Life	P 25

Autumn

Curious and Free	P 27
Beyond the Sea	P 28
Back Where I Came From	P 30
The Art of Living	P 31
It is Raining Outside	P 32
Sweet Alison	P 33
Changes	P 36
Sea of Sadness	P 38
The Cat's House	P 41
A Poem in Miniature	P 43
Darkness	P 44
100 Years	P 45
A Sense of Emptiness	P 46
Lullaby of a Turning Stone	P 48

Winter

Bitter Lemon	P 50
To Her	P 52
Of Lovers	P 53
To the West	P 55
The Other Side of the Door	P 58
Summer or Not	P 60
Wishes	P 62
To Someone who Left no Sign	P 64
All and Nothing	P 67
This Life	P 68
Summer Wind	P 70
Christmas	P 72
The Last Circuit	P 73
Wishing for Life	P 74

Summer

The Lady Waits	P 77
Togetherness	P 80
For your Eyes	P 82
The Velvet Part of the Moon	P 84
Fantasia	P 86
Candlelight	P 88
A Moment like This	P 91
The Soul and the Moon	P 92
Diamonds	P 93
Poem to Vincent	P 95
Stay Here	P 97
Waking in Spring	P 99
Your Infinity	P 101
To Jill	P 102

Spring

When all is fresh and new and treasures wait to be discovered.

The Flight of a Seagull

A deserted beach
>   where you can imagine
>>   what happens out at sea

stars in the sky
>   eyes glowing in the dark
> they appear to stare
>>   to make you wary

my thoughts
>   journey far away
> much too far to follow

now I am alone
>   solo in time
perhaps for a while
>   perhaps for just a moment

it seems a bit curious
>   or even strange
>   how at certain times
>   you have a sensation
>>>   of loneliness
>   an emotion

that sometimes
can offer relief

I feel something strange in the air
I feel something uncertain in the air
yet I cannot understand
if it is the wind
or a dream

out of the dark a light suddenly shines
a lone seagull
uncertain where to go
a seagull who is unique
with an unusual expression
he has something to say
but cannot speak
and like me
he cannot sleep
he just keeps flying
with no fixed destination

twisting curves in the air
      diving at the sea
    barely touching the surface
      before rising again

now a bit weary
      wishing to rest
    he lands swiftly on a rock
    out at sea

a solitary wave
      that does not comprehend
    drags him off
      and drowns him

the stars in the sky
      appear dimmed
    at the unhappy fate
      of an innocent seagull

and the stars in the sky
      are dimmed
    at the unhappy fate
      of an innocent seagull

Invisible Hand

Building

      the explosion is powerful

 an invisible hand is writing things for me

I don't want to stop it

    I don't want it to stop

 I can't stop it

    I can't control it

instinct

 red

   primeval

     moving

       increasing

     above everything

    building

  destroying

lighting a fire of pure essence

  there the next day

    the day before

      belonging to the day after

    and after that

     again

      and again

moving down the page

     writing

looking for the quickest way
behind it everything is brief
everything is new
leaving a trail of fire
blazing down to the sea
sizzling
and laughing
or is it crying

now
all is quiet

When the Sky is Calm

Certainly
  living here
    pastels are no longer any use
here
  scenes that pass and go
being is what I have
  asking questions of yourself
       or shutting yourself in a cage
  leaving messages on photographs
here
   windows thrown wide to the sun
      what there is

lights that light up the dark
   angels are born
where the sky rests
  only in this way
and when the sky takes a rest
      I too will rest
it is only when the sky is calm
       I will rest

and only silence will remain to talk to me

The Part Shadowed by the Sun

From the extremes of this night
   the widening part of the sun
     slowly
    is leaving
between the forks of branches

I am walking
 in the part shadowed by the sun
dark
   like a white page
when the moon does not know what to say
   and Sunday is still so faraway
I never remember the first
    and always forget the next
  at the confines of time without limit
and define love
   tired of the lines
    from smiling and crying
and journeys of thoughts
   towards a sleep that eludes
    on a pillow creased by life
   listening
to sweet telepathy

Night Time

Night
 twin souls
   restless
   heart intuitive and perverse
glow of the dew
     shadow of the moon
who are you shining for

night
  like black high heels
      never a headache
   talking about me
the smell of asphalt
     or reinforced concrete
why

night
  like a sad smile
    like a sweet lament
still water
      never knows torment
how come

night
 my eyes of autumn
        watch time being consumed
they know about me
   the taste of this place
when

night
 a kiss with no forgiveness
   a kiss for a long wait
 the kiss of a closed door
   the kiss of a light left on
why and for who

night time
        for this night of stars

Dear Old Story

Dear old story
                    every time I hear you
I would like to laugh at your words
but every now and again I still cry
I wonder if I ever understood you

dear story
             tell me who you are
you always laugh but you never have lines
and when you cry you are never sad
are you by any chance the queen of clowns

my story
             you have never been written
and I would like to read you
I would like to know you
to love you
I would like you to help me fly
on your clear pages
clear as water
     as air
         as the sun
give me water
         air

and sun

give me life

maybe mine is just a dream

but I want to shout to you that I won't stop dreaming

and my shout will reach you

as clear as water

air

the sun

I love you so much

dear old story of mine

I Know

Now I am alone
   alone and waiting
time is not important
      time is infinitive like us

I know it will happen
   and will bring seasons with sweet fruit
     and it will also bring water
        transparent and brightly coloured
  and it will bring life
   a life without end
holding it up
   keeping it safe
     embracing
      impressions of love

I know it will happen
     I am not sad
    I am simply waiting
      like eternity
       do not mistake
   I am not unhappy
    I am waiting
I know it will happen

When the Sun Shines

When the sun shines
  it envelopes the branches of memory
    life passes
   but is not that serious
      spirals of sound vibrate in the air
and like the air
    I am not afraid
when the sun shines
      it opens your heart like a rose bud
      and like a rose
  I feel no pain
  I can dance with my shadow
everything is in motion
        because everything changes
  shy and fresh

the first drops bring the rain
  I watch it sliding slowly down my greenhouse
    and the rain will kiss my lips
  the rain will wash the earth
it will rain until the end
    and then the sun will return
      and reduce all war to ashes
  and there will be peace

a peace that does not yet exist in history books
and it will be the sun that heals this fragile earth
and from the earth this morning
a flower was born in my garden

When

When flowers rest
  to be more beautiful next day
when you will no more see waves
  breaking on cliffs
when a smile and a tear
  will no longer have any importance
when you see the stars
  reflected on the sea
when the present and past along with the future
  will no longer have limits
when you will no more have noise
  disturb your senses
when solitude
  will frighten you no more
in that moment
  you are listening to your soul

Tell Me About You

While your soul embraces my dreams
     I look for a place to lay down my problems
how I don't want these tears
    they don't ask to be let out
             but they will escape sooner or later
          as the rain doesn't perceive barriers
    and knows where to go
cathedrals of light
       illuminate me
         embracing me in spirals of use
and while I wait for your voice
       I will sing for silence
but it has never been easy
you are all the colours of the wind
  undress slowly
     looking around you
princess of fables
  I feel good
  as long as I talk to you
    it is enough for me
             to talk about you

Something is There

Clouds above me
>
the smell of the sea beneath me
>>
sounds of a life far away behind me
>
and in front of me
>>
light gliding on water

coming neither from sky nor sea
>
a light out there

when there is no moon and no stars
>>
but the alternative
>>>
I cannot accept

amazing
>
something is over there
>>
but I don't know what it is

I listen awhile and hear something
>>
that comes from neither sky nor sea

a light that shines
>>
now I know what it is

inside me
>>
an immense peace
>>>
that is
>>>>
within me

My Seasons

I see the moon embrace
      a ray of sun
  and I hear the rain dancing
        on passing time
  a red leaf is waiting
    to fall in flight
fragile elf on a branch
    plays music for you
I glimpse white coming gently to rest
   on a tree lined avenue
   smoke rising
  and evaporating
        frolicking
as a result of the cold
   and I hear a silence painted with
   a thousand shades
 that bring a thousand seasons
far away
  and I see colours
    searching for a rainbow
  swallows
   open the sky to happiness
I listen to life playing
  on fields gowned in flowers

and like a light sleep
yesterday's friend
and lazy white clouds
pierced by the sun
talking of stories kindled by
the light of love
waiting
like the ring
I gave you
shining
like diamonds
waves in the sea
speaking to me
about you
your dreams

tell me
why you were laughing
what you are like
what you were like

Colours of Life

Painting is a dance
                        of undefined time and mystery
            a song of poetry
                        and rhythm
a piece of the artist's soul

 dreams not yet slept
        words still to be said
            thoughts unspoken
                ideas to realise
                    wishes
                        even now to hope for

a rainbow of colours
                        and imaginings
obscurity
        mixed with precision
                        and depth
the song of a mermaid

Autumn

Summer is over - taking the bright colours with it, but winter has not yet arrived.

Curious and Free

Just like a Venetian blind
     a sliver of light comes in
  just like a cat
free
  and curious
    inquisitive
  like a cat
curious and free

free
  from guns of plastic
    of metal
      of thoughts

not where curiosity
   and understanding
  are lost
as they grow
  in a river of people
    diluted
  a day of freedom
and curiosity

just like a free and curious cat

Beyond the Sea

It is already morning
   and you cannot comprehend
      the same doubt still remains
why is it only the ship of your dreams
      that can take you beyond the sea

how often at night
   have you lain in bed
      staring at the ceiling
      asking yourself
why you cannot change this life
   a boat that takes on more water with every second
how hard it is to stay afloat
      and then
         what about work
            some consolation prize

years have gone by
      and nothing has changed
because it is only the ship of your dreams
      that can take you beyond the sea

all those friends
   have gone away

never getting in touch
    already forgotten
you have nothing left
    except two strong hands
        now playing the guitar
as you try to understand
    if it is only the ship of your dreams
        that can take you beyond the sea

dear friend
    these words I wished to dedicate to you
                    are of no use at all
I wrote them
    simply to help you understand
it will only be the ship of your dreams
    that will take you beyond the sea

Back Where I Came From

Talking

    talking

        and saying nothing

 listening

    listening

        and hearing nothing

 looking

    looking

        and yet seeing nothing

  thinking

    thinking

        and not understanding

a smile

    no one sees it

I set my face straight again

        everything in place

  and return where I came from

The Art Of Living

I feel it doesn't reflect anything
but there is a mirror inside that talks to me
everything seems to be normal
however I never know what is behind the mirror
I take things seriously
but since that time
I don't take them anymore
I love life everyday
fully knowing it won't love me
and I look for the best
even though I don't know what it is
I hear mermaids sing
that old love song you never hear anymore
and I listen to a distant voice
saying
the art of living
is living with art
art is living

Is It Raining Outside

The curtains are drawn
    the cat is still
I no longer hear the notes
    the circle must be finished
I lie on my bed
    switch off the light
    but I can't sleep
    or even think
    I can no longer see life
I switch on the light again
    and also the radio
    hoping for an idea

the leaves of my plant are yellow
    books covered by dust
    are full of history
soulfully alone
    the telephone is quiet
    an ashtray waiting for another cigarette
    I only have three left
    I want to go out and buy them
    but

who knows if it is raining outside

Sweet Alison

Sweet Alison
is the name of the boat
a single thought
I must not go back
arid land
without hope
just like the journey
he is about to undertake

with no destination any more
his life
is like that great cargo
already his house
his world
goes from stern to aft
clean air
he can only find again in port
the guitar
to be able to sing
those choruses
that make him think
and then Whiskey
to forget
that woman

he can no longer love

a mouth
with no more words
a beard
that no longer has an owner
hard work
that is killing him
and takes him
to the point of desperation
money is now
his god
having no ideals to follow
and no family
to think about
having no sentiments
to leave

the only friend left
is a parrot
who repeats constantly
go home
run to look up your friends
your girl
your town

he finds people
 willing not to remember
   that one day
    he too knew how to love
     that he ran
      like others under the sun
       between weeping willows
       in the courtyard

     sadness is now
      at the bottom of his heart
     it sticks into him
    without peace
   he knows
 what is the most important thing
 but it is already time to cast off

       how many seas to cross
      how many women to love
     without love
    how many dreams lost
   in an instant

Sweet Alison is the name of the boat

Changes

So

 the rain falls

   is it curiosity

      or

        vertigo

and then

  I watch eternity slide down the window

                        it never seems to tire

   who knows why

   it is raining outside

I look for shelter

 once

   again

 it is easier to die

    then to change

  change

it takes forever

  to remove

    only

      one grain of dust

so
when shoes are too tight
you are then forced to change
when

it is raining outside
I will breathe
the ability
and desire
to live

Sea of Sadness

You see them coming back

                from the same sea

  you see the same boats coming back

      you see the same faces coming back

unloading sweat on the pier

his colleagues watch him

      they shake their heads

they smile at the moon

      the night of a party

he's big enough

      but it is bravery he lacks

he looks at the sea

      but appears not to see it

short trousers

      play on the beach

        the looks of the people

      pockets full of nothing

reflections of the sea
    smell of salt
he thinks about tomorrow
    lines on his face

the window
    the only one he remembers
        when he looked at the sea
        and his eyes
            were full of hope

the sea
    always the same
yours
    and theirs
that sea
    that now
        he doesn't care about

calm sea
    full moon
today
    also passed
        like the day before

no smile

    heart tired

    afraid of leaving at night

 afraid

of not coming back

        in the morning

    the same as the day before

also today

    a star cried for him

The Cat's House

She isn't here
who knows where she is
the cat's house
is inside her
open the door
on the eyes of the world
to filters of light
on precious stones

with small steps
and the steps are many
small steps
but soft

she isn't here
who knows where she is
the cat's house
is inside her
like thoughts
mystery
like something orange
in the sky

a rest while sleeping

but when it moves
it really moves

she isn't here
who knows where she is
the cat's soul
is inside her

A Poem in Miniature

I wanted to welcome you
                wide world
        but somehow I never could

the less success I had
                understanding you
the more I wanted you

I did not understand
        I did not know
                you were there

it was here amongst the little signs
        I should have started

now I know
    I did not know how to love you

now I understand
        I was unaware I loved you

Darkness

The day has been siphoned into darkness
  a man prepares his eyes for the night
    his hands clasp anguish
      rapidly advancing
        in darkness that wounds everything
          even his shadow is hiding
            a voice set in motion
            words fall from dreams
              wake up darling it is tomorrow already
              I have to go but
you can remain if you want

100 Years

Sumptuous legs
   finely cut
      nice figure
         perfect line
            a bit too ornate
      tasteless grace
   nearly vulgar
valuable no doubt
   one hundred years of history
         in a classic piece of furniture
         in Baroque style
   without a doubt causing regret
to observe and comprehend
   its one hundred years of rings
reduced to cabinets

A Sense of Emptiness

You should not believe
      in a wizard's shadow
    sitting on the edge
     of a patched up nest
   you are drowning
     in a sea of sand
  and from the fireplace
     no smoke is coming out

you
  do not hope for divine justice
      because as far as vine goes
    there is only a full glass
true words
   words of fire
     but what is left
is only a sense of emptiness

just like now
   that big lawn
     that one day
       was in flower
         with forget-me-not
my love

time is past
       and you well know
    that the Robin I gave you
is still waiting
   sitting beside
           that wizard's shadow
but it is
           only a sense of emptiness

Lullaby of a Turning Stone

Walking through life
   people are resentful
        jealous of my happiness
I have many things to do
     although little time
       and this trepidation
  sweet and nervous
     takes me
       carrying me away
looking inward
    for myself
       it is as if the world never ends
my strength
    the fear inside me
  bears me on its wings
      to carry me over cities
    above the roofs of houses
  onto tired old geography
and reserved spaces
      in this world without personality
while I sing myself
        the lullaby of the stone that turns

Winter

Darkness descends with grey skies and dull days.
The few short hours of light are not enough to
illuminate the way.

Bitter Lemon

One two three

            four legs

as the chair

            darling

is wooden

      and if there were three

one two three

           four lights

                  I know

     probably too many

        who knows

horrible that colour

            bitter lemon

   but if it were another

                 it would be sweet orange

a sip at a time

     I kiss the coffee

   careful not to err

           as then I would kiss you

that painting is off centre

        just like me

   but I do not care

        as I drink lemon tea

for you are here now
        but I know you will go
  close the door quietly
            you know how

I am still me
    even without you
  misanthropy
          yes
  no
    lights and coffee
I am me
    and I think for myself
 people are boring
    all prêt-a-porter

useless love
    without poetry
        I will shut outside
I will drink coffee

To Her

I went to her with my tired arms
   towards her
 I hadn't made love to her
      for many years
  not since
   with the last kiss
 she said to me
I love you

I
 afraid
  ran away
 I don't have the courage to look back
  I know I would see the ruins of Pompeii
 falling on my shadow
  on this road
   wet from the rain

I no longer have the courage to go near her

 she
  oozes hate from every pore

I don't want to get dirty

Of Lovers

Now you
 a wet pink knife thrust
then us
 my dreams are born
   from signs of lies

you
 cloud in a sky that is not there

you and I
 words cut in half
  water with no bridge
us

so much searching to loose ourselves
 and the constantly asking
  what is love
learning to love the limits
 loving the limitations

you have become
 rose coloured electric barbed wire
we have
 no laughter about any of these things

we lose something everyday
    and ask ourselves again and for always
        what is love

you
    sincerely
        no

To the West

Faces I can see
   that come and go
      inside the people
  if there are any
while life
      is here and there
  between mirrors
   that speak to me
the west
   still in my mind

even my dreams
   demand more now
gentle incidents
      and then
  deviations and pauses follow
   further on

to soar at this point
   I don't know
on this glass
  I can't manage
      to feel
  but

nevertheless
　　　　it manages to cut
right through my heart

in the meantime
　　December falls
　　　　on the people
　　　　　who linger
when I cross my fingers

I listen to the voices of life
　　　no
I can't halt it

even my eyes
　　open a bit more
　　　　　with each passing day
as if they were flowers

　　I will take the time
　　　　　left to me
　　　　　　to stop everything now
　　　　　　　I don't know

in my hands
        only my mind remains
    in the west

but in the meantime
        December progresses
    on the people
        going towards the exit
            I will breathe life
and no
    I won't stop it

The Other Side of the Door

I am speaking softly so I cannot be heard
on the other side of the door they are eavesdropping

I am whispering because I am afraid of the dark
if they found out it would be the end of me
when I was a child this made me cry
now as an adult all that remains is regret

I am speaking faintly with a soft voice
on the other side of the door they are listening to me
on the other side of those mountains
 a friend is waiting for me
with thirty pieces of silver to spend together
and there I saw love
but it was too big to hold in my arms
I opened my arms to a blasphemy
closing my heart to a minor wrong
the nights in May when I was young
I saw the women getting ready together
and it is May again yet I cannot hear their voices
maybe they are praying in silence
so as not to be heard

I will speak in an undertone
in the silence I see them die
I switched off the light so as not to be seen
my fear of them sweeps away my fear of the darkness
on the other side of the door are all my friends
who when night falls are not to be trusted
in the middle of the night they start to scream

Summer or Not

Books
    full of dust
        idle
history
    full of lies
telling yourself you will change
    is to believe in believing
convenience
    or stupidity

how difficult it is not to hear
    the will not to hear
        the will not to understand

continuing
  is no help
the rain
    knows
  humidity
    authority

when time does not change
    maybe the ability is absent

summer
        or not
it is definitely war
        little or big
    but
whatever it is
        war is there
here
        inside me

Wishes

Mummy

do you care about your son

mummy

please please play with me

mummy

I don't want to grow up

as I am afraid of the dark

I don't want to grow up

as I am afraid I will no longer be sweet and tender

mummy

where were you on Christmas day

where were you when I was ill

where were you

when I was dying with the desire to fly

mummy

I won't let money fall out of my pockets

anymore

as I don't want the gypsies to carry me away

mummy

I will clean my shoes every morning

will you then wait for me

when I come home late at night

mummy

I will be good for you

I will marry her and she will be wearing white
I don't want to go off to war
but I am still dying to fly
mummy
why can't I feel you close like my hands
mummy
why can't I feel you close like my eyes
mummy
why can't I feel you close like my breath
like the perfume from the flowers I gathered for you

mummy
who or what is the dark you tell me about
who or what is the light you never tell me about

in my garden a flower is dying to fly

To Someone who Left no Sign

Look at all the lights
           how they sparkle
    they are not shining for us
                anymore

reflected on calm water
              they dance on a dream
                     that is no longer there

with only one gesture
                you are going to kill them
     recollections that remain

this darkness surrounding me
    takes me back
          to emotions I have already felt

I will carry into the distance
                 anything I no longer need
       besides
           in your eyes
               my words
                  are only embers of something gone

you never speak to me

       you never did speak to me

turning away

    no decision made

        searching for someone to replace me

    no answer given

living like this

    within meaningless barriers

      simply grows more exhausting

here with me

      close

   and yet not present

I am uncomfortable

    at the idea of you staying

I will wipe out your lies

       but you

    loose the taste for me you have acquired

I will carry into the distance
　　　　everything you never were
　　the things I gave you
　　　　cannot be bought
　　　　　you will not have a chance
　　　　　　　to be offered them again

you no longer exist
　　　　there never was
　　　　　　　a you

All and Nothing

Unquestionably
          I ask for nothing
but my shoes
          hurt all the same
I worked hard
     to find my stride
dull colours
      a sunny house
forgive me my God
       for these wrong keys
the day a slap in the face
     the night a whisper
         a crumb on the ground
           a sin too many
       I will take the car
a road
  a fork
     left
      right
        a pole in the middle
forgive me my God
     for this mistaken life

This Life

Pieces of life like this

                              that's all there is

    water that salts coffee

here

    I live here

men yell

        and shove

they never stop

      I no longer feel anything

    powerful the silence

I don't have

rising up a little

    you can see what there is

                     if it is there

pieces of life like this

        that's what there is

   pieces of a life that is mine

no

    they are never enough

       they are no longer enough

this life I have

      this life no

            this life

   I want this silence

Summer Wind

I no longer feel red lips
but rather the fire of a dream in my hand
about you and a good painting
perfect notes with time and words

now I do not know what to think
with the doubts
and voices which seem strange

maybe you too are running quickly
in the night I wish to dream

I dream it is a dream
and none of it is true
I dream you are still here
with your colours of precious stones
and may your pain rest

and I feel your journey on the edge of the sun
with its light
but there is nothing to be done

now you are in my hand
like a new day so far away

now you
a world that is silent
a faded flower is all that remains

tell me if you have a kiss for me
you who talk of love
but where is your heart

tell me if your shadow
has a secret passage to lead me to you

you flew away with the summer wind
eyes closes and light wings

between pine needles
and the sea's waves
stealing from my heart
nights of love
you flew away without a word
because my eyes had cried

then out of the blue
I hear I love you
I saw your eyes
and it was Christmas

Christmas

Christmas in the eyes of a child

eyes that reflect other eyes

    for ever so distant

and hide whoever is near them bearing presents

    eyes of a child

full of tears not yet fallen

    eyes that know nothing

           and yet quiver

eyes that don't love whoever is near them

    the eyes of a child

        who is about to embark on a journey

            from which he cannot return

eyes of a child who doesn't understand

            why he can't understand

    not seeing why he can't hear

eyes of a child that will never grow up

      because the effort is greater than him

eyes of a child from whom life was stolen

    who in the soul of his hand

        holds on tight

           to a pencil the form of a heart

so he can draw the world

        and design dreams

            as old as time

The Last Circuit

Autumn awaits the falling of leaves
        when the sun is altered
  and I remember
           a Christmas tree
that will be lit for little more time
        just like the lights in the windows
  before total darkness
the thought is old
        older than man
  the railroad track is antiquated
   where the train of life
          is making its last rounds
   with the end of the line to hand
 stories consumed
      then put aside
curved sticks
  well aged
    with the patience of existing
   between silence and noise
I hate to see children grow old

Wishing For Life

I am still here
the road forks
I don't know
I am breathless
the price of life is high
and so
my dreams lie in fragments
I won't pick them up
they cannot be put together again
I don't know
I am only a man
feeble and ineffective
but I won't give up
a step
and yet another
on and on
life is like a river bed
waiting for rain
and it will go
I feel it going
it rises with the wind
and I know it will bring me life
occasionally ashes

      sometimes sun

   but I will not give up

  it builds in strength

   like a river gathers force

and I won't give up

  no

   I will not give up

Summer

Flowers bloom and the sun turns the many hues of colour into shining rainbows filled with hope.

The Lady Waits

It is here she is waiting
but this is just another time
she has dressed carefully
in joy and hope
as she is still awaiting a dream
amongst the never ending smoke
in the same club

with her green eyes
that denude her thoughts
waiting for other eyes
she saw just yesterday
and beyond that fog
too thick to cut
appear those eyes
sweeter than love itself
so deep and true
it shakes her inside

she lets them in
like leaves in the wind
seeing them
as if they were made of sun
seeing that look

her resistance melted
it is all in her head
and she has in mind strange thoughts
she would like to let them fly
like a rose bud opening in spring

it is all so simple
and plainly true
that when she sees white
it replaces black
between the musicians and the smoke
she holds on tight to that moment
the notes change
and the rock becomes a slow dance
and now she knows
she no longer has control
she moves slowly
and asks for this dance

that is how together
breast touching breast
they keep in step with the dance
and that is how time
feels like drops of water
and that is how their lips met

love is an intensity of riches
and only it does not lie
it is in the depths of her heart
and is the only thing she feels

Togetherness

Every day and every night
there's a flower in my mind
that is not so far away
when you hold my hand
it's another perfect day

when I look into your eyes
I can feel you pull away
why are you so unsure
you can decide tonight
while tomorrow is mine

when you embrace me you enrich my heart
fail me and even I may fall apart
tonight

there is a part in all of us
that's a little insecure
which I need you to embrace
make me feel secure
hold me in your arms

bear in mind that tiny part
that's a little insecure

which I don't want you to hurt
take away my pain
stay with me tonight

if you don't worry and leave the day behind
whatever happens
it will be all right
tonight

For Your Eyes

This is why I am here
   beneath this sky
that is never still
     beside a far from calm sea
       your skin full of stars

and this is why I am here
   surrounded by green
        to say these three words to you

that is why I said yes
   anything for your eyes

when we hold each other like this
   the cold no longer frightens me
let's love each other like this
   in the rain falling on us
for your eyes
      I wish to die only here
   for this night
     that has your eyes

this is why I am here
   to dress your hair in rose red fire

    to listen to your voice
and this is why I am here
  one step away from the world
    a world not yet ready for you
for you I said yes
      for your eyes
              anything

let's hold each other like this
   and there is nothing left that hurts
let's love each other like this
   in a moment that lasts for ever
for your eyes
          yes
      for you I said
              yes

The Velvet Part of the Moon

Wandering alone
  on a solitary beach
        wandering alone
              on the shore
  I heard a man
            laughing and shouting at the moon
  foolish and fearless
        enjoying his angry sea
over the stillness
        of a crystal pool
    never broken
        by a stone cast in
I heard a whisper
  calling the endless skies
          sweeping away
      the noises of the earth
          all the greys in the tones
    like a snowflake lights
            the darkness of my mind
      the wildness of my thoughts

when the mistral comes from the north
    a new wind turns

       its madness into a gentle breeze
full of promises and fables to be told
as passing by
   the lonely castle wall
      I saw the King's ruthless hand
  freeing sweetly
         his favourite white steed
      stroking and soothing
            the velvet muzzle shone
   a twinkle in his eyes
the wizard shifts the curtains to the world
        lilies and roses strewn on the floor
    where children are playing a new wise game
  taught to them by storytellers
         who dance and play
      living in a flame
   and then the shadows
        will turn to glowing shapes
full of promises and fables to be told

Fantasia

I will quietly count
　　but only up to six
if I close my eyes and look behind
　　　I will find you there

　I see you dressed
　　in clouds and sky
　flowers in a book
　　I read every night

I may be fragile
　　but my thoughts never are
　they drive the rainbows of my mind

Fantasia you play with my thoughts
　　bringing them life
　　　　in this dream I wish to live

I will marry
　my heart and your soul
　　　and in silence
　　　　I will fly on your wings

　I will follow you

through sky and clouds
  far away from thoughts
and beyond
 I will escape with you

Candlelight

Dance
the flame dances
we find ourselves alone
and naked
in this room

dance
the flame paints patterns of light
our eyes closed
searching for your essence

by candlelight
I will give you my heart
in a circle of light
circle of breath

by candlelight
you will give me love
shadow of a rose
vase of diamonds

the light that you are
the light that you give

you are still dancing
you never tire

dance
the flame dances
a ray from the moon
shining in this room

dancing
your ballet
is a leaf of light
sensations of elegance

by candlelight
a spell
transports us
into the eyes of a sunset

candlelight
simply your name
only the flame
has no discord

dancing for us
   the flame dances
      choosing the rhythm
  flowing around

dance
  the flame dances
    dance for us
  alone in this room

A Moment Like This

For a moment like this
    I created a road that leads to paradise
for a moment like this
    I transformed the notes of a song
                into a falcon's flight
       I counted each wave in the sea by night
for a moment like this
    I sculpted diamonds hidden in a dream
            so they gave more light
      I exchanged my heart for a rainbow
for a moment like this
    there is a place in the sunlight of my dreams
          where I sit on summer evenings
    with you
because
    for a moment like this
        I painted love
    and it has your eyes

The Soul and the Moon

Through a smile without age
    the moon is already with her
and with a hand in hers
    she will never leave
the moon will dance for her
    and she knows she will not sleep
the white rays
      the words
of a code never written
    awaiting her
playing on the wings of her smile
    until dawn takes her unaware

my soul
    now you are here
      still inside me
I will not leave you
    and I will read to you each night
      tale of a love that is rare
between the soul and the moon

Diamonds

And you
   gold thread without end

   and us
my dreams are born
      in immense eyes alive with blue

and you
   sun in a sky of diamonds

   and us
words of love without age
     water at sunset
       and us

how we looked to find us
  never asking ourselves
       what is love
loving the imperfections
  the imperfections

and then you
  rose
    dressed in emotions

and then us
     our hands tremble
  our lips search

we look for and find something new everyday
    without having to ask ourselves
                what is love

and you
  and us

sincerely

Poem to Vincent

(dedicated to Van Gogh)

This is simply a song
    born in my thoughts
and written in a prison
       where I died yesterday

to those of you
    who listen to me now
and hear these fragile notes
      if my words open the door
           to the soul that you have
then you will have understood
    what I am trying to tell you
and when my mind
    does not exist in a desert
it navigates freely in an open sea

I paint clowns and Pierrot
    in my mind
loving this life that
  sometimes
    does not hear me
but I hear it

I will sing you a poem
  I will sing about my life
do not ask me if God exists
    I myself do not even know
but I do paint rainbows
      even when the sky is hazy

I paint clowns and Pierrot
    in my mind
leaving this life that
  now
    does not hear me

and I do not hear

Stay Here

Stay here
    near me
  with your fragility
those memories
    are not you
  hold me like this
      and they will follow you no more

stay here
    near me
  as if we were in harmony
let yourself go
  if you want
 stay here
  and you can rest
     your eyes in mine

if your hands tremble
    there are hands that will warm them
  if you want

stay here
    near me
an angel is missing

it is you
who narrates its poems
about you
you never talk about you

stay here
if you want
stay here
or I will miss you
I will not ask you for more
I will not ask you
if your heart is inside mine

and if winter comes back
you are the summer that will go on for ever
if you wish

Waking in Spring

Like air that comes to rest
  on the glow of a flame
       the flame lights up
    at the radiance of your face
     a star in the desert
    that illuminates my soul
and your spirit alights
  on petals from roses

like ears of corn in the wind
     then the wind takes a break
  a rest that is gentle and carefree
      above powder from the snow
and like snow beneath the sun
     unafraid of the heat
   I will sleep without fear
  since your dreams are by my side

how sweet is your smile
     that has never asked for anything
   and I have said nothing to you
     before these words
  and without you these words

would not be a song

without you this song

would not be about love

this love is unguarded

and will never be able to say enough

it only takes one word

and that word is simply sorry

I am truly sorry my love

too often unsaid

I feel like a wave

the beach has spirited away

letters never written

then left on the cushion

that space so empty

it makes me feel alone

I hear the melody of a violin

sing a song of poetry

it is your song that calls me

to wake me in the evening

it is your aria that calls me

to wake me in spring

Your Infinity

Suspended on the extreme limits of uncertainty
     I envisaged infinity from the horizon
in that moment
   not big enough for me
          and beyond the ocean of sentiments
      I saw your eyes
   reflected on the sea
but they were bluer and deeper
   so far and yet so near
      they called to me
         irresistibly
like the song of mermaids

  I didn't feel alone
      but oh that solitude
      and I cried
    a dive to reach you
     and my tears
       merged sweetly
         in the friendly water of the sea

To Jill

What is a diamond
    if it hasn't your name written on it
       only a stone with no light
while you
      will shine forever